LIFE IN THE BALANCE
Exercises in Ethics

By

Paul Holland

ISBN 978-0-9722059-6-2
Published by:
SWG Marketing LLC   Little Falls, NJ
Life in the Balance - Exercises in Ethics copyright 2010 by Paul Holland
all rights reserved

Important Note:

This work is intended solely as a tool to assist in promoting healthy discussion and debate in the area of personal ethics. It is intended to aid individuals and groups in the development of ethical thinking practices. It is not a substitute for personal judgment as each real life situation is different and should be approached as such.

The scenarios for discussion are fictional, designed to address aspects which simulate real life moral dilemmas which might occur. Often such decisions in real world situations may incur legal ramifications and in those instances prudent, competent professional advice should always be sought.

Any resemblance to actual persons, places or occurrences is purely coincidental.

Dedication:

To my father, who was always there for us.

Foreword:

The subject and substance of ethics has been debated for thousands of years.

But the necessity for ethics has never been in question.

In recent years we have seen time and again the results of what a lack of ethics has wrought on our society and our planet.

I found it ironic that after the Enron debacle, there was an outcry demanding to know why we no longer require ethics to be taught in business school. I would humbly submit that by that time, ethics would merely be an academic exercise. By the age of twenty, your moral compass was long ago hardwired. Trying to impress values then would simply be closing the barn door long after the horse is gone.

Our ethical decision making and resultant behavior both good and bad is something that we learn from the cradle. Just like anything else, to improve we must work at it. If we train ourselves to rationalize bad behavior and make excuses for our actions, regardless of how heinous they may be - we get better and better at making unethical choices. That is how storm troopers and robber barons are made – one unethical decision at a time. History has shown there is nothing more inhuman, than someone who used to be human.

Conversely – if we train ourselves individually to view the problems that confront us from the standpoint of a strong moral compass, collectively we get more ethical outcomes, because it is habit. Making sound choices becomes second nature. The best part is that such a society is more profitable, more stable, less contentious and more benign to all its citizens. How we approach ethics individually is a measure of how we will as a society approach them collectively.

How to use this book:

This book works best by putting the scenarios out to small groups of about 10 or 12 so that different viewpoints can be expressed.

There is no specific order or logic as to how the scenarios are listed. They have been purposely jumbled.

The group leader or facilitator should screen the scenarios so that they can insure the content is appropriate for the age and makeup of group.

The leader or facilitator and group members should encourage full participation by withholding judgment on the contributions of participants. Particularly with young people, they will occasionally be purposely contrarian in an effort to be amusing or to dare authority. When that happens, without being confrontational, ask the group, "Is that really what you think? Is that a serious ethical answer?" Ideally, group discussion and participation should always lead the members to find ethical solutions collectively. Seeing this peer reasoning will assist individuals to follow similar pathways on their own and strengthen their ethical problem solving skills. It may also encourage participants to speak with others when they are faced with problems that are value based.

10 points to help make ethical decisions

- We accept personal responsibility for our choices.
- Will my action or inaction harm anyone or anything?
- Does it take into account all that will be affected?
- Are any punished or rewarded unjustly?
- Is our motivation based on truth, fairness and reason?
- Does it serve the greater good?
- Does it sacrifice the future for an immediate goal?
- Are you proud of your decision?
- If the roles were reversed, would you be satisfied?
- How can my decision be reversed or remedied if I'm wrong?

If you have trouble answering these questions, maybe your answer is in question...

#1: We accept personal responsibility for our choices.

The very essence of ethics centers in our ability to recognize our personal responsibility for our choices.

We live in an era when everyone seems consumed by what their "rights" are. As a result, the process by which we make decisions is almost exclusively based on how we will be affected individually rather than collectively. We think short term. We shout about rights, to disguise our wrongs. We seek to deflect our responsibilities.

In short we live in the age everyone is quick to point fingers but when they point at us we cry, "It is nobody's fault." What utter nonsense.

You can see the result all around us. Waning natural resources, gross over-consumption, greed, corruption, apathy...

This is what happens when we ask, "Is it legal?" rather than is it just, moral and true? We leap through loopholes without regard for the ramifications. But such things have a habit of catching up with us. Invariably when we fail to behave ethically, we sow the seeds of our own destruction.

Changing this path is not easy and it is often uncomfortable. It begins with taking personal responsibility for our choices and accepting the consequences that follow. Ultimately we become the sum product of the choices we make. When we think that way and take ownership of the outcomes - we do a better job of choosing wisely and well.

It begins by saying, "Yes, I am responsible for the decisions I make."

#2: Will my action or inaction harm anyone or anything?

Virtually everything we do has consequences, good and bad.

Simply because I cannot or choose not to see who might be injured as the outcome of my actions does not alter the fact that others may be paying the penalties for things I have done or failed to do.

For example: I buy a pair of shoes made by slave labor half a world away. I may know this happens but have no knowledge that this is the case with regard to this particular product. If I choose to look the other way, remain ignorant and continue to buy those shoes –my inaction/apathy helps perpetuate the practice. If someone informs me that this particular shoe company engages in this practice but I really like the shoes and the price so I choose to buy them anyway, my action supports the continuation of the practice.

An ethical person must reasonably ask; who or what may sustain harm as a result of what I do or fail to do? It may not be a person directly. It may be a nameless and faceless entity such as a company, group or the environment. We like to forget at times that such entities are comprised of people. So regardless, when we collectively look the other way we endanger ourselves and our society, because when we are the injured party, who will hear us?

An ethical person seeks to do no harm.

#3: Does it take into account all that will be affected?

Nothing happens in a vacuum.

Ethics is not a series of isolated incidents; it is a system wherein we understand that every action must have a reaction. Often it is not possible or even reasonable to take all of the ripple effects of our decisions into account but certainly we should take the time to recognize the primary consequences of what we do.

Depending on the gravity and magnitude of our decisions, it is our onus to drill down to see secondary and tertiary effects as well. We need to predict the ripple effect or suffer the consequences.

An ethical person understands that our decisions often affect more than just ourselves.

#4: Is it fair – are any punished or rewarded unjustly?

In accepting personal responsibility for our actions, we also must accept the consequences for our mistakes. When we are wrong we are obliged to do what is required to make amends. When we fail to admit to our mistakes and seek to make reparations, we compound our error.

Along those same lines, if you would not wish to be punished unjustly, why would you wish to profit from others unjustly?
Caveat emptor – Let the buyer beware. That should not be a license to cheat and steal from the unknowing. Ethical people recognize that such a system protects us all at one point in time or another. In an ethical society – there is justice for all. In an unethical society – there is justice for none.

The ethical person wants only that which he has justly earned. He doesn't want or expect others to pay for his mistakes and when he does err – he seeks to set it right.

#5: Is our motivation based on reason, truth and justice?

We are all human and subject to the frailties that come with the package. Greed, jealousy, apathy, anger, fear... The list is almost endless, yet – we are capable of rising above these base instincts.

When faced with a moral dilemma, take time to understand the basis of your decisions.

Ethics is a highly unusual dish because it must be prepared cold and served warm. Our decisions must be grounded in reason, stripping away the virulent, knee jerk passions that too often surround important choices in our lives. Hot heads rarely create sound outcomes. The ultimate litmus test however is to place ourselves in the position of the other affected parties. It is invariably then that compassion and understanding are able to season our reason.

The ethical person would not do to others that which he would not want done to himself.

#6: Does it serve the greater good?

It would be so much simpler if all decisions were just black and white – good and bad... but they rarely if ever are. In fact, the more important a decision the more sticky and convoluted it generally seems to be.

That does not reduce our need for ethics – it should increase our reliance on them. It is using these simple tests for the relative "correctness" of a thing that will allow us to shave away at the layers which disguise the truth.

When we are faced with tough decisions, it is often because there may not be a way for all parties to emerge unscathed from a difficulty but that does not excuse us from doing the best we can with what circumstances we are given.

There may not always be a "perfect" outcome but there should always be an ethical one.

#7: Does it sacrifice the future for an immediate goal?

Immediate goals are usually not well considered.

Asking ourselves about the future ramifications of our actions is often the first, best way to examine how valid our choices are. It is because we stop thinking about what we want for a minute and consider instead what we truly need. A wise farmer doesn't eat his best corn. He saves that for next year's planting. In this way his crop only gets better over time.

Everything comes with a price. When we give some thought to what it is we are truly trading away in the future for what we are getting in return now, it often gives us reason to pause.
Some of our most precious assets are things like reputation, integrity, respect, honor, trust… They can take a lifetime to build and a moment to destroy.

It is said that time is our most precious possession because it is the one thing you can never get more of. That being said – who would trade one moment for all their future moments? Ethical decisions stand the test of time.

The ethical person knows they forge their future one sound decision at a time.

#8: Are you proud of your decision?

Would you be justifiably proud if others learned of your actions and decisions?

Think of people whose ethical opinions you value and respect. It could be anyone: family members, teachers, religious figures, co-workers, friends...

Would you be content to lay the problem at their feet, secure in the knowledge that they would find how you handled it admirable?

At the end of the day, if in your heart you "hope no one finds out" you already know the answer to this question.

Ethics should never fear the scrutiny of others.

#9: If the roles were reversed would you be satisfied with the decision?

The litmus test of fairness is that you would never do something to another, that you would not want done to you.

Often people will attempt to rationalize what they know to be wrong. "He got what he deserved." – or – "The insurance will cover it." – or – "It is not my problem."

Rationalization is rarely rational.

People look for excuses because they need them. They know what they have done is less than ethical and consequently they feel the need to justify and explain their behavior, if only to themselves.

Put yourself, personally into the position of being the recipient of the consequences of your decision, your behavior, your action or inaction…

Notice what the title question does not say. It does not ask if we would be pleased with the decision – only if we would be satisfied.

Ethics must be weighed in a balance and a balance tips both ways.

#10: How can my decision be reversed or remedied if I'm wrong?

We are all capable of making a mistake.

Sometimes even the best intentioned decisions or actions can go awry. In examining our ethical decision making process for example; we may exercise our best judgment in a situation only to learn later that our facts were incomplete. Perhaps we might misinterpret a set of circumstances, allow strong emotion to temporarily cloud reason or give credence to some information that was in error.

It hardly seems fair that there is only one optimum solution and so many ways to be mistaken or confused.

This is all the more reason to weigh our response to a moral dilemma carefully - particularly when we seek to judge the responses of others. Given their circumstances we might be driven to the same conclusion they came to.

One of the best ways to do this is to ask the question, what if I am wrong? What does the remedy look like? In some cases there is no way to reverse your actions. Take the drastic case of putting a prisoner to death. There is no way to undo that. Consider the simpler and more common problem of saying the wrong thing. Once a thing is said, you may apologize but you cannot "unsay" something. That sting could last a lifetime.

Taking time to consider how we might recover if we are wrong opens the door to recognizing our own fallibility.

It allows us to second guess ourselves, long before we may need the remedy.

The Scenarios

- We accept personal responsibility for our choices.
- Will my action or inaction harm anyone or anything?
- Does it take into account all that will be affected?
- Are any punished or rewarded unjustly?
- Is our motivation based on truth, fairness and reason?
- Does it serve the greater good?
- Does it sacrifice the future for an immediate goal?
- Are you proud of your decision?
- If the roles were reversed, would you be satisfied?
- How can my decision be reversed or remedied if I'm wrong?

SCENARIO #1

A man is a near perfect donor match for his sister who needs one of his kidneys to avoid a lifetime of dialysis. She is 47 years old, the mother of two teen age sons and works in an office in a nearby city.

The man is also a high probability match for a famous scientist, who is a poor candidate for dialysis. The scientist is 74 years old, never married but his unique research in the area of alternative energy generation is considered very promising.

You may assume that both potential organ recipients are in otherwise good health for their age.

Should the man donate one of his kidneys – and to whom?

- *We accept personal responsibility for our choices.*
- *Will my action or inaction harm anyone or anything?*
- *Does it take into account all that will be affected?*
- *Are any punished or rewarded unjustly?*
- *Is our motivation based on truth, fairness and reason?*
- *Does it serve the greater good?*
- *Does it sacrifice the future for an immediate goal?*
- *Are you proud of your decision?*
- *If the roles were reversed, would you be satisfied?*
- *How can my decision be reversed or remedied if I'm wrong?*

SCENARIO #2

A man has just been fired from his job without any warning or severance. He had been employed as a salesperson at a retail jewelry store but due to the slow holiday season that just ended he was terminated by the new manager to save money.

He had been a good worker for 12 years at this company and has a wife and child to help support. Others at the store who had kept their jobs are paid less than he was.

When he protested the manager as much as hinted the reason he was being fired was that things had gone missing and there was a suspicion he had been stealing. He warns him to accept his termination and leave quietly or he may be accused.

While walking home, the man sees a small bag from the store where he had worked containing several very expensive pieces of jewelry that someone has dropped.

How should he do next?

- *We accept personal responsibility for our choices.*
- *Will my action or inaction harm anyone or anything?*
- *Does it take into account all that will be affected?*
- *Are any punished or rewarded unjustly?*
- *Is our motivation based on truth, fairness and reason?*
- *Does it serve the greater good?*
- *Does it sacrifice the future for an immediate goal?*
- *Are you proud of your decision?*
- *If the roles were reversed, would you be satisfied?*
- *How can my decision be reversed or remedied if I'm wrong?*

SCENARIO #3

A man wishes to sell his car and someone he works with wants to buy it.

They have been employed by the same company for 8 years but work in different sections. They do not socialize.

The prospective buyer is 32 years old, married with 3 small children and things are little tight financially. He needs the car to get to work and transport his family.

The seller is 62, married with one grown child. He wanted to retire soon but economic conditions have eroded what he and his wife had set aside for the future. He wishes to replace the car with one that will last him and his wife for many years.

The car is 7 years old and looks great but has recently been making an unusual noise occasionally. The seller is a little concerned it may develop a serious problem.

What should the seller do?

- *We accept personal responsibility for our choices.*
- *Will my action or inaction harm anyone or anything?*
- *Does it take into account all that will be affected?*
- *Are any punished or rewarded unjustly?*
- *Is our motivation based on truth, fairness and reason?*
- *Does it serve the greater good?*
- *Does it sacrifice the future for an immediate goal?*
- *Are you proud of your decision?*
- *If the roles were reversed, would you be satisfied?*
- *How can my decision be reversed or remedied if I'm wrong?*

SCENARIO #4

A single woman has been dating a man who seems to be her ideal match on every level. Their relationship is beginning to become more serious now, to the point where they are both contemplating marriage.

Both are in their late twenties, neither one has ever been married before. However, while still in her teens the woman had been arrested and pleaded no contest to a shoplifting charge. Because she was a minor – the case record is sealed.

Her prospective fiancé works as a security guard and is studying law at night. He has had run-ins with juvenile delinquents in the course of his job several times. Twice he has had to defend himself and he is not at all sympathetic on the subject of youthful offenders and gangs.

Should she tell him about her past?

- *We accept personal responsibility for our choices.*
- *Will my action or inaction harm anyone or anything?*
- *Does it take into account all that will be affected?*
- *Are any punished or rewarded unjustly?*
- *Is our motivation based on truth, fairness and reason?*
- *Does it serve the greater good?*
- *Does it sacrifice the future for an immediate goal?*
- *Are you proud of your decision?*
- *If the roles were reversed, would you be satisfied?*
- *How can my decision be reversed or remedied if I'm wrong?*

SCENARIO #5

A woman is hired to manage an office with 82 employees. After she has been there for a month, she notices someone she thinks she knows working as a security guard. He had been her former boss in another company 15 years earlier. At that time he had been a heavy drinker and had often bullied her and her fellow employees. His explosive, angry tirades were frequent and often unexpected. He was always demeaning and verbally abusive. He fired her best friend there over a trivial matter that wasn't even her fault.

Although she liked her old company, she was very glad when she found another job and was able to quit just to be rid of him.

His employment file confirms it is the same man. He has been working here now for 9 years in security and has a spotless record. Outwardly, he seems completely changed and there has been no indication that he has recognized her.

How should she proceed?

- We accept personal responsibility for our choices.
- Will my action or inaction harm anyone or anything?
- Does it take into account all that will be affected?
- Are any punished or rewarded unjustly?
- Is our motivation based on truth, fairness and reason?
- Does it serve the greater good?
- Does it sacrifice the future for an immediate goal?
- Are you proud of your decision?
- If the roles were reversed, would you be satisfied?
- How can my decision be reversed or remedied if I'm wrong?

SCENARIO #6

A young, recently hired engineer at a manufacturing company takes it upon himself to perform quality control tests on different fasteners that they use in their products. He finds that all of them are substandard according to the specifications of the original design.

From what he can see, these are the same fasteners, from the same supplier that they have been using for years. They are much less expensive substitutes than the fasteners which are indicated in the design.

To date, they have not contributed to an injury or warranty field failure that they are aware of.

What should he do?

- *We accept personal responsibility for our choices.*
- *Will my action or inaction harm anyone or anything?*
- *Does it take into account all that will be affected?*
- *Are any punished or rewarded unjustly?*
- *Is our motivation based on truth, fairness and reason?*
- *Does it serve the greater good?*
- *Does it sacrifice the future for an immediate goal?*
- *Are you proud of your decision?*
- *If the roles were reversed, would you be satisfied?*
- *How can my decision be reversed or remedied if I'm wrong?*

SCENARIO #7

After being out of work for 9 months, a man 34 years of age gets job as a day laborer at a construction site.

The company has a strict policy forbidding any drinking during working hours for safety reasons. Despite this fact, his foreman and the rest of his small work gang frequently have lunch at a bar and grill nearby the work site and will usually have one beer with their meal.

He always feels pressured to join them. He worries that he may anger his foreman if he does not but he is also concerned that they flaunt the ban on alcohol, even though no one seems to enforce it. Either way, he needs this job and is concerned about losing it.

How should he proceed?

- *We accept personal responsibility for our choices.*
- *Will my action or inaction harm anyone or anything?*
- *Does it take into account all that will be affected?*
- *Are any punished or rewarded unjustly?*
- *Is our motivation based on truth, fairness and reason?*
- *Does it serve the greater good?*
- *Does it sacrifice the future for an immediate goal?*
- *Are you proud of your decision?*
- *If the roles were reversed, would you be satisfied?*
- *How can my decision be reversed or remedied if I'm wrong?*

SCENARIO #8

A woman is carefully considering how she might vote in an upcoming election.

There are two candidates running for office.

The voter likes and agrees with the platform of the first candidate on almost every position that he stands for, however on one key issue that is very important to the voter the man is diametrically opposed.

Both she and the candidate strongly consider their respective positions in this matter one of conscious (even they hold opposing views).

Conversely she disagrees with the second candidate on almost everything except that he is a staunch supporter of her pet cause.

How should she use her vote?

- We accept personal responsibility for our choices.
- Will my action or inaction harm anyone or anything?
- Does it take into account all that will be affected?
- Are any punished or rewarded unjustly?
- Is our motivation based on truth, fairness and reason?
- Does it serve the greater good?
- Does it sacrifice the future for an immediate goal?
- Are you proud of your decision?
- If the roles were reversed, would you be satisfied?
- How can my decision be reversed or remedied if I'm wrong?

SCENARIO #9

The star/captain of the school football team is in trouble.

Despite having been warned repeatedly that he must pull up his grade in math, he has ignored opportunities for extra help and study to focus on the upcoming "Big Game". He knows that performing well will help insure his chance at a scholarship to college.

Now days before the game, he has failed yet another big test. When the teacher publishes these scores it will make him academically ineligible to play. He will be forced to sit on the bench. This is the last game of his high school career. The school will probably lose the game without him and he will certainly lose any opportunity at his scholarship.

How should they proceed?

- We accept personal responsibility for our choices.
- Will my action or inaction harm anyone or anything?
- Does it take into account all that will be affected?
- Are any punished or rewarded unjustly?
- Is our motivation based on truth, fairness and reason?
- Does it serve the greater good?
- Does it sacrifice the future for an immediate goal?
- Are you proud of your decision?
- If the roles were reversed, would you be satisfied?
- How can my decision be reversed or remedied if I'm wrong?

SCENARIO #10

A man loves fishing, it is his passion.

He has for years sought to catch "Big Jake" a monster fish that is supposed to reside in a remote lake only accessible by a mile long foot path. The lake has a strict catch and release policy. All catches must be returned unharmed to the water.

Local people all know stories about the legendary fish but the majority of them consider "Big Jake" to be no more than a myth.

On one hot summer afternoon, the man manages to land "Big Jake". However, he is alone and has no way to verify his capture other than carrying him back to town which would surely result in the death of the trophy fish. He knows that no one will ever believe him without proof and in fact if he tells anyone, they will probably mock him.

What should he do?

- We accept personal responsibility for our choices.
- Will my action or inaction harm anyone or anything?
- Does it take into account all that will be affected?
- Are any punished or rewarded unjustly?
- Is our motivation based on truth, fairness and reason?
- Does it serve the greater good?
- Does it sacrifice the future for an immediate goal?
- Are you proud of your decision?
- If the roles were reversed, would you be satisfied?
- How can my decision be reversed or remedied if I'm wrong?

SCENARIO #11

A 14 year old teenager is trespassing in an abandoned factory. He has been warned against going here by family and friends but on a dare, he scaled a locked fence and broke a window to gain entrance.

His goal is to find some small item that will prove to the others that he has been inside.

While in the darkened building, he witnesses two men in their twenties (one of whom he knows) hiding a bag. He waits until after they leave to investigate and finds the bag which contains a large quantity of money and a loaded hand gun.

What does he do next?

- We accept personal responsibility for our choices.
- Will my action or inaction harm anyone or anything?
- Does it take into account all that will be affected?
- Are any punished or rewarded unjustly?
- Is our motivation based on truth, fairness and reason?
- Does it serve the greater good?
- Does it sacrifice the future for an immediate goal?
- Are you proud of your decision?
- If the roles were reversed, would you be satisfied?
- How can my decision be reversed or remedied if I'm wrong?

SCENARIO #12

A doctor has been forced to retire from his very lucrative surgical practice after having been sued for medical malpractice.

Even though he was exonerated, the stigma of the trial ruined his reputation and cost him his hospital privileges causing him to go into research. Because he no longer practices medicine he does not need or carry malpractice insurance.

Now the young daughter of the attorney who had prosecuted the case against him in court is gravely ill and may not live out the night. The ex-doctor is the only one with the knowledge and skill necessary to give the child a fighting chance but at best there is only a 50% chance she will live. If the little girl does survive the operation, there is also a 50% chance she will suffer some brain damage.

What does the doctor do?

- *We accept personal responsibility for our choices.*
- *Will my action or inaction harm anyone or anything?*
- *Does it take into account all that will be affected?*
- *Are any punished or rewarded unjustly?*
- *Is our motivation based on truth, fairness and reason?*
- *Does it serve the greater good?*
- *Does it sacrifice the future for an immediate goal?*
- *Are you proud of your decision?*
- *If the roles were reversed, would you be satisfied?*
- *How can my decision be reversed or remedied if I'm wrong?*

SCENARIO #13

A man is on trial for committing multiple violent murders during the course of a robbery. The six victims were bound and gagged. They were executed just to eliminate potential witnesses.

A police officer realizes during the course of the trial that the prosecution has failed to disclose some key evidence that might contradict their theory of the case and cast doubt as to the man's guilt. If brought forward at the trial, it might prevent the conviction but if brought to light afterward an attorney might get the lower court's ruling overturned on appeal and man would go free. With double jeopardy attached, he could never be retried for the crime again.

He is certain the man on trial is guilty.

What does he do now?

- *We accept personal responsibility for our choices.*
- *Will my action or inaction harm anyone or anything?*
- *Does it take into account all that will be affected?*
- *Are any punished or rewarded unjustly?*
- *Is our motivation based on truth, fairness and reason?*
- *Does it serve the greater good?*
- *Does it sacrifice the future for an immediate goal?*
- *Are you proud of your decision?*
- *If the roles were reversed, would you be satisfied?*
- *How can my decision be reversed or remedied if I'm wrong?*

SCENARIO #14

A woman works in a bakery.

At the end of the day, all of the baked goods that are not sold are thrown out in their dumpster.

Three blocks away is a struggling soup kitchen that could really use this food, however the bakery owner is adamant that the leftovers at the end of the day must be disposed of. He donated the excess production in the past and it resulted in a lawsuit once. For this reason is unwavering in his orders that all baked goods not sold must be destroyed each day.

The woman lives in an apartment that overlooks the soup kitchen and she would like to help, but simply cannot afford to contribute time or money because of her long hours and modest salary.

What should she do?

- *We accept personal responsibility for our choices.*
- *Will my action or inaction harm anyone or anything?*
- *Does it take into account all that will be affected?*
- *Are any punished or rewarded unjustly?*
- *Is our motivation based on truth, fairness and reason?*
- *Does it serve the greater good?*
- *Does it sacrifice the future for an immediate goal?*
- *Are you proud of your decision?*
- *If the roles were reversed, would you be satisfied?*
- *How can my decision be reversed or remedied if I'm wrong?*

SCENARIO #15

While standing in an alley, a homeless man witnesses a purse snatching out on a busy street.

The victim is very well dressed and appears wealthy.

The robber runs right past the homeless man and scales a fence at the end of the alley. In the process, he accidently drops the purse and he sees if fall into a small space behind some trash.

The police are in hot pursuit. They are stymied by the fence but radio for backup to try to catch the thief at the other end of the block. They were not in time to see the purse drop so no one knows it is there but the homeless man and the thief.

Both the homeless man and the thief are somewhat similar in appearance.

What should he do?

- *We accept personal responsibility for our choices.*
- *Will my action or inaction harm anyone or anything?*
- *Does it take into account all that will be affected?*
- *Are any punished or rewarded unjustly?*
- *Is our motivation based on truth, fairness and reason?*
- *Does it serve the greater good?*
- *Does it sacrifice the future for an immediate goal?*
- *Are you proud of your decision?*
- *If the roles were reversed, would you be satisfied?*
- *How can my decision be reversed or remedied if I'm wrong?*

SCENARIO #16

A volunteer is collecting money for the poor, standing outside a local store. The man gives a few hours a day to help out this cause because while he is unemployed, he has more time than money to contribute himself.

The man is an avid coin collector and notices that among the handful of change that a donor just dropped in, there is a very rare quarter that could be worth hundreds of dollars.

He could easily exchange it for one of the quarters in his pocket.

What should he do?

- We accept personal responsibility for our choices.
- Will my action or inaction harm anyone or anything?
- Does it take into account all that will be affected?
- Are any punished or rewarded unjustly?
- Is our motivation based on truth, fairness and reason?
- Does it serve the greater good?
- Does it sacrifice the future for an immediate goal?
- Are you proud of your decision?
- If the roles were reversed, would you be satisfied?
- How can my decision be reversed or remedied if I'm wrong?

SCENARIO #17

A couple owns a small shop that is struggling in tough economic times.

In counting the day's receipts, they discover that someone has passed them three counterfeit $100 bills. In good times this kind of a loss would be difficult to adsorb, now it is crushing.

If they bring them to the bank or the police, the bills will be confiscated and they will receive no restitution. If they take them to a large store and attempt to pass them on – they will probably get stopped by a cashier using some means of fraudulent bill detection. They must either take the loss or attempt to pass it on to other small business owners like themselves.

What should they do?

- *We accept personal responsibility for our choices.*
- *Will my action or inaction harm anyone or anything?*
- *Does it take into account all that will be affected?*
- *Are any punished or rewarded unjustly?*
- *Is our motivation based on truth, fairness and reason?*
- *Does it serve the greater good?*
- *Does it sacrifice the future for an immediate goal?*
- *Are you proud of your decision?*
- *If the roles were reversed, would you be satisfied?*
- *How can my decision be reversed or remedied if I'm wrong?*

SCENARIO #18

A twenty year old man is brought to the emergency room of a small local hospital. He had been drinking, ran off the road while driving and struck a tree. He was not wearing a seat belt and suffered multiple injuries including severe head trauma.

By the time he reached the hospital he had stopped breathing twice in the ambulance and after extended efforts each time the EMT crew had managed to restore a heart beat. Now as he enters the hospital, his heart and lung functions cease again. He is without oxygen to the brain for another 7 minutes when at last, a faint heart beat is detected.

Given all the damage that has resulted, there is a better than 99% surety that he will remain in a persistent vegetative state for many, many years on artificial life support with virtually no hope of recovery.

What happens next?

- We accept personal responsibility for our choices.
- Will my action or inaction harm anyone or anything?
- Does it take into account all that will be affected?
- Are any punished or rewarded unjustly?
- Is our motivation based on truth, fairness and reason?
- Does it serve the greater good?
- Does it sacrifice the future for an immediate goal?
- Are you proud of your decision?
- If the roles were reversed, would you be satisfied?
- How can my decision be reversed or remedied if I'm wrong?

SCENARIO #19

A brilliant young computer programmer is hired to write a sophisticated piece of software for a client as a freelancer. They agree to a 50% deposit, with the balance paid after the satisfactory delivery of the product.

After the code is up and running the company refuses to pay the balance stating that they want to make certain the program is operating "as promised" and once they are completely satisfied, she will receive the balance of her money. Two more months go by without payment.

The company is unaware that the programmer inserted a "backdoor" in the code that would permit her to access their mainframe in the event the client refused to pay. If she sabotages the code, it will shut down the company computers and idle thousands of workers.

What should she do?

- *We accept personal responsibility for our choices.*
- *Will my action or inaction harm anyone or anything?*
- *Does it take into account all that will be affected?*
- *Are any punished or rewarded unjustly?*
- *Is our motivation based on truth, fairness and reason?*
- *Does it serve the greater good?*
- *Does it sacrifice the future for an immediate goal?*
- *Are you proud of your decision?*
- *If the roles were reversed, would you be satisfied?*
- *How can my decision be reversed or remedied if I'm wrong?*

SCENARIO #20

In school, one young man listens while he hears another blatantly lie about a girl in their class.

He knows that the assertions made by his classmate are false because at the time of the alleged incident, he had seen her quietly studying at the library.

The fellow making these false statements is very popular and the gossip is already spreading. He is afraid that if he exposes the lie it may backfire and his schoolmates will choose to believe the other person rather than him.

What should he do?

- *We accept personal responsibility for our choices.*
- *Will my action or inaction harm anyone or anything?*
- *Does it take into account all that will be affected?*
- *Are any punished or rewarded unjustly?*
- *Is our motivation based on truth, fairness and reason?*
- *Does it serve the greater good?*
- *Does it sacrifice the future for an immediate goal?*
- *Are you proud of your decision?*
- *If the roles were reversed, would you be satisfied?*
- *How can my decision be reversed or remedied if I'm wrong?*

SCENARIO #21

The line of customers is very long and moving slowly. The service counter is understaffed. The only person currently manning it is a young woman who is doing her best to handle each problem thoroughly under difficult conditions. It is fairly evident that she is relatively new to the position.

The people waiting are becoming increasing impatient and irate. Finally the person behind you on line launches into a long, loud and bitter diatribe of complaints, criticizing the store, the lack of efficiency, the employees and this particular clerk's efforts.

He then looks at you for approval.

What do you say?

- We accept personal responsibility for our choices.
- Will my action or inaction harm anyone or anything?
- Does it take into account all that will be affected?
- Are any punished or rewarded unjustly?
- Is our motivation based on truth, fairness and reason?
- Does it serve the greater good?
- Does it sacrifice the future for an immediate goal?
- Are you proud of your decision?
- If the roles were reversed, would you be satisfied?
- How can my decision be reversed or remedied if I'm wrong?

SCENARIO #22

A commodity trader is very troubled by certain market barometers that he believes make buying very risky at this time, such that he would not invest his own money.

However he receives no salary from his company - only commissions for executed trades and despite what he is seeing, his firm has issued a buy recommendation.

He knows several clients that might be ready to get into the market, but thinks they might lose their money if they do...

What should he do?

- *We accept personal responsibility for our choices.*
- *Will my action or inaction harm anyone or anything?*
- *Does it take into account all that will be affected?*
- *Are any punished or rewarded unjustly?*
- *Is our motivation based on truth, fairness and reason?*
- *Does it serve the greater good?*
- *Does it sacrifice the future for an immediate goal?*
- *Are you proud of your decision?*
- *If the roles were reversed, would you be satisfied?*
- *How can my decision be reversed or remedied if I'm wrong?*

SCENARIO #23

A man leaves his car for an oil change at a local service station that has just opened up. When he drives away afterward he notices the car is making a noise that he never noticed before.

He returns to the station where a mechanic examines the car and tells him that the necessary repairs will cost over $1500. He recommends that the car should not be driven.

He doesn't remember hearing the noise before bringing the car in for service but he cannot be certain.

What should do?

- *We accept personal responsibility for our choices.*
- *Will my action or inaction harm anyone or anything?*
- *Does it take into account all that will be affected?*
- *Are any punished or rewarded unjustly?*
- *Is our motivation based on truth, fairness and reason?*
- *Does it serve the greater good?*
- *Does it sacrifice the future for an immediate goal?*
- *Are you proud of your decision?*
- *If the roles were reversed, would you be satisfied?*
- *How can my decision be reversed or remedied if I'm wrong?*

SCENARIO #24

The foreman at a small company has a dilemma.

He has been told he must lay off three out of the eight people who work in the shop.

Frankly, one of the least productive workers is also one of his oldest friends, the same man who had originally helped to get him hired at the company.

After the lay off, to keep up with the workload everyone who remains will have to be as productive as possible just to keep up.

What should the foreman do?

- We accept personal responsibility for our choices.
- Will my action or inaction harm anyone or anything?
- Does it take into account all that will be affected?
- Are any punished or rewarded unjustly?
- Is our motivation based on truth, fairness and reason?
- Does it serve the greater good?
- Does it sacrifice the future for an immediate goal?
- Are you proud of your decision?
- If the roles were reversed, would you be satisfied?
- How can my decision be reversed or remedied if I'm wrong?

SCENARIO #25

A girl in high school tells a friend in strictest confidence that she is concerned about another student.

She claims that the other girl has gotten in over her head with a bad crowd; shoplifting, drugs, drinking... In addition, her falling grades and problems at home have this other girl contemplating suicide.

The friend wonders if this "other girl" might not be the one doing the talking.

What should the friend do next?

- We accept personal responsibility for our choices.
- Will my action or inaction harm anyone or anything?
- Does it take into account all that will be affected?
- Are any punished or rewarded unjustly?
- Is our motivation based on truth, fairness and reason?
- Does it serve the greater good?
- Does it sacrifice the future for an immediate goal?
- Are you proud of your decision?
- If the roles were reversed, would you be satisfied?
- How can my decision be reversed or remedied if I'm wrong?

SCENARIO #26

A girl has been asked out to the movies by someone she knows her parents would not approve of.

She likes this person who is several years older that she is and has the ability to drive.

She normally goes to the movies anyway with friends on the weekend and might even run into this person just by chance.

What should she do?

- *We accept personal responsibility for our choices.*
- *Will my action or inaction harm anyone or anything?*
- *Does it take into account all that will be affected?*
- *Are any punished or rewarded unjustly?*
- *Is our motivation based on truth, fairness and reason?*
- *Does it serve the greater good?*
- *Does it sacrifice the future for an immediate goal?*
- *Are you proud of your decision?*
- *If the roles were reversed, would you be satisfied?*
- *How can my decision be reversed or remedied if I'm wrong?*

SCENARIO #27

A college freshman football player on an athletic scholarship is told to drop a class in his major because it will interfere with an hour of practice twice a week.

His declared major is more demanding than that of any of the other players. He will need this class to take others within this field of study and he will need all of these courses to stay in his major and graduate in four years.

When he protests he is told, "You are here to play football. Drop the course or lose your scholarship."

What does he do?

- We accept personal responsibility for our choices.
- Will my action or inaction harm anyone or anything?
- Does it take into account all that will be affected?
- Are any punished or rewarded unjustly?
- Is our motivation based on truth, fairness and reason?
- Does it serve the greater good?
- Does it sacrifice the future for an immediate goal?
- Are you proud of your decision?
- If the roles were reversed, would you be satisfied?
- How can my decision be reversed or remedied if I'm wrong?

SCENARIO #28

While taking care of the next patron in line, a cashier suddenly realizes that on the previous transaction he made an error and had short changed one of their regular customers by ten dollars.

The customer generally comes in at least once or twice a week and both cashier and customer know each other by name.

The store is very busy so the cashier cannot leave and the customer has already walked away.

What does the cashier do next?

- We accept personal responsibility for our choices.
- Will my action or inaction harm anyone or anything?
- Does it take into account all that will be affected?
- Are any punished or rewarded unjustly?
- Is our motivation based on truth, fairness and reason?
- Does it serve the greater good?
- Does it sacrifice the future for an immediate goal?
- Are you proud of your decision?
- If the roles were reversed, would you be satisfied?
- How can my decision be reversed or remedied if I'm wrong?

SCENARIO #29

While taking care of the next patron in line, a cashier suddenly realizes that on the previous transaction he made an error and had short changed one of their regular customers by ten dollars.

The customer generally comes in at least once or twice a week and both cashier and customer know each other by name.

The store is very busy so the cashier cannot leave and the customer has already walked away.

> Suddenly the customer returns with the manager accusing him of purposely cheating him saying this has happened before, even though that is not true.

What does the cashier do now?

- *We accept personal responsibility for our choices.*
- *Will my action or inaction harm anyone or anything?*
- *Does it take into account all that will be affected?*
- *Are any punished or rewarded unjustly?*
- *Is our motivation based on truth, fairness and reason?*
- *Does it serve the greater good?*
- *Does it sacrifice the future for an immediate goal?*
- *Are you proud of your decision?*
- *If the roles were reversed, would you be satisfied?*
- *How can my decision be reversed or remedied if I'm wrong?*

SCENARIO #30

A builder is running way behind schedule and way over budget on a job. Bills are mounting and the customer is complaining.

One of his suppliers calls. They cannot supply the concrete that has been specified for two more days, further delaying the job.

He can get an inferior grade of material which also will cost less delivered today. Switching to the substitute would probably never be noticed.

What should he do?

- *We accept personal responsibility for our choices.*
- *Will my action or inaction harm anyone or anything?*
- *Does it take into account all that will be affected?*
- *Are any punished or rewarded unjustly?*
- *Is our motivation based on truth, fairness and reason?*
- *Does it serve the greater good?*
- *Does it sacrifice the future for an immediate goal?*
- *Are you proud of your decision?*
- *If the roles were reversed, would you be satisfied?*
- *How can my decision be reversed or remedied if I'm wrong?*

SCENARIO #31

Your supervisor has made a serious blunder that almost cost the company one of their largest customers.

When the president of the company storms in and demands an explanation, your supervisor openly blames you for the fiasco but assures the president that he has handled the problem, states that you are an otherwise good worker, that you will be re-trained and that it never happen again.

Seemingly satisfied, the president leaves.

Your manager then pulls you aside and tells you that you must "take one for the team" and if you refuse, he will see to it that you are fired with cause making it difficult or impossible to find another job in this industry.

You need this job, what do you do?

- *We accept personal responsibility for our choices.*
- *Will my action or inaction harm anyone or anything?*
- *Does it take into account all that will be affected?*
- *Are any punished or rewarded unjustly?*
- *Is our motivation based on truth, fairness and reason?*
- *Does it serve the greater good?*
- *Does it sacrifice the future for an immediate goal?*
- *Are you proud of your decision?*
- *If the roles were reversed, would you be satisfied?*
- *How can my decision be reversed or remedied if I'm wrong?*

SCENARIO #32

Your favorite place to meet with friends to eat and relax has been slowly changing.

A new group of regular customers have started to frequent the establishment who are rather loud, obnoxious and demanding.

They tend to drink far too much and become rowdy. They often use language, tell off color stories and jokes that you find very offensive. This had always been a quiet family oriented place in the past.

The owner is torn because the new people spend a lot of money in his establishment, but he sees his regular clientele becoming more and more agitated.

What should you do?

- *We accept personal responsibility for our choices.*
- *Will my action or inaction harm anyone or anything?*
- *Does it take into account all that will be affected?*
- *Are any punished or rewarded unjustly?*
- *Is our motivation based on truth, fairness and reason?*
- *Does it serve the greater good?*
- *Does it sacrifice the future for an immediate goal?*
- *Are you proud of your decision?*
- *If the roles were reversed, would you be satisfied?*
- *How can my decision be reversed or remedied if I'm wrong?*

SCENARIO #33

You are school age boy living at home. You see a man walking along with a cardboard box containing three small kittens.

You stop to look at them and comment on how cute they are. The man tells you to take good look because he is taking the box to the pound to have them euthanized.

Your parents are adamant about not having any pets. If you bring even one of them home, you know they will be furious with you.

What do you do?

- *We accept personal responsibility for our choices.*
- *Will my action or inaction harm anyone or anything?*
- *Does it take into account all that will be affected?*
- *Are any punished or rewarded unjustly?*
- *Is our motivation based on truth, fairness and reason?*
- *Does it serve the greater good?*
- *Does it sacrifice the future for an immediate goal?*
- *Are you proud of your decision?*
- *If the roles were reversed, would you be satisfied?*
- *How can my decision be reversed or remedied if I'm wrong?*

SCENARIO #34

The president of a small company is facing a dilemma.

He has a potential investor that wishes to take a significant position in his company. The company needs this infusion of cash not only to weather hard economic times but to seize some very real opportunities that could lead to significant growth in the future. The problem is that to get the investor to come in the president must relinquish a great deal of control. In return for his investment, the man wants two seats on the board of directors and to replace both the chief financial officer and the director of marketing with his people. The president is also aware that in at least two other companies, this investor was instrumental in closing plants and moving everything off-shore.

They have always been a family operation and a key local source of employment.

Does he make the deal?

- *We accept personal responsibility for our choices.*
- *Will my action or inaction harm anyone or anything?*
- *Does it take into account all that will be affected?*
- *Are any punished or rewarded unjustly?*
- *Is our motivation based on truth, fairness and reason?*
- *Does it serve the greater good?*
- *Does it sacrifice the future for an immediate goal?*
- *Are you proud of your decision?*
- *If the roles were reversed, would you be satisfied?*
- *How can my decision be reversed or remedied if I'm wrong?*

SCENARIO #35

An attractive, popular high school senior has not studied for their math final. They need a good grade or they may lose their acceptance into the college of their choice.

The class "math geek" is very shy and quiet with no social life to speak of.

Should this less than studious but very popular senior befriend the mathematical classmate and to what degree?

How should our resident "math wizard" respond?

What do you think?

- *We accept personal responsibility for our choices.*
- *Will my action or inaction harm anyone or anything?*
- *Does it take into account all that will be affected?*
- *Are any punished or rewarded unjustly?*
- *Is our motivation based on truth, fairness and reason?*
- *Does it serve the greater good?*
- *Does it sacrifice the future for an immediate goal?*
- *Are you proud of your decision?*
- *If the roles were reversed, would you be satisfied?*
- *How can my decision be reversed or remedied if I'm wrong?*

SCENARIO #36

A young man is studying to be a mortician. His family has owned a local funeral home for two generations.

He meets a young lady, enrolled at a local teaching college and the two hit it off immediately. They have a great deal in common, but he is concerned that his somewhat unusual chosen profession may be something of a shock and turn off for his new found interest.

All she knows is that he is a student.

What should he do?

- We accept personal responsibility for our choices.
- Will my action or inaction harm anyone or anything?
- Does it take into account all that will be affected?
- Are any punished or rewarded unjustly?
- Is our motivation based on truth, fairness and reason?
- Does it serve the greater good?
- Does it sacrifice the future for an immediate goal?
- Are you proud of your decision?
- If the roles were reversed, would you be satisfied?
- How can my decision be reversed or remedied if I'm wrong?

SCENARIO #37

A young woman applies for a waitressing job at a restaurant. The manager is very impressed with her and is prepared to offer her the job but then she is informed that she must be 21 because they are part of a big franchise chain and they serve alcohol on the premises.

The state they are in only requires that she be 19 to serve alcohol by law, but the policies of the company are more restrictive.

She looks much more mature but will not turn 21 for another 9 months and she really wants this job because they offer full benefits.

What should she do?

- *We accept personal responsibility for our choices.*
- *Will my action or inaction harm anyone or anything?*
- *Does it take into account all that will be affected?*
- *Are any punished or rewarded unjustly?*
- *Is our motivation based on truth, fairness and reason?*
- *Does it serve the greater good?*
- *Does it sacrifice the future for an immediate goal?*
- *Are you proud of your decision?*
- *If the roles were reversed, would you be satisfied?*
- *How can my decision be reversed or remedied if I'm wrong?*

SCENARIO #38

You and your best friend decide to attend the same university. During rush week, you find the ideal fraternity and you both decide to join but there is a problem.

They want you – they don't want your friend.

Now, what do you do?

- *We accept personal responsibility for our choices.*
- *Will my action or inaction harm anyone or anything?*
- *Does it take into account all that will be affected?*
- *Are any punished or rewarded unjustly?*
- *Is our motivation based on truth, fairness and reason?*
- *Does it serve the greater good?*
- *Does it sacrifice the future for an immediate goal?*
- *Are you proud of your decision?*
- *If the roles were reversed, would you be satisfied?*
- *How can my decision be reversed or remedied if I'm wrong?*

SCENARIO #39

The office manager is interviewing people for a technical sales position that has opened up. Several very strong candidates have been in. Three in particular had very impressive resumes, years of extensive industry experience and were very professional in how they presented themselves. Each one interviewed very well at length. All of them were willing to work for the range of compensation offered and could begin immediately.

The manager just hired a recent college graduate with no experience that you know of after a 5 minute interview. His degree is not in a related field. He is to start at the same salary and compensation that you receive currently, but you have working for the company for three years. Now in addition to your existing duties, you are expected to train him.

You know for a fact that the new hire regularly attends the same small church as the manager.

What do you do?

- We accept personal responsibility for our choices.
- Will my action or inaction harm anyone or anything?
- Does it take into account all that will be affected?
- Are any punished or rewarded unjustly?
- Is our motivation based on truth, fairness and reason?
- Does it serve the greater good?
- Does it sacrifice the future for an immediate goal?
- Are you proud of your decision?
- If the roles were reversed, would you be satisfied?
- How can my decision be reversed or remedied if I'm wrong?

SCENARIO #40

Two families have been neighbors for over 15 years. Both have enjoyed a comfortable, upper middle class lifestyle.

Eight months ago that changed when one of the two men became unemployed. His wife works two jobs but it has been a struggle economically. Despite this fact, the man never seems to be actively seeking work.

To help out, the other neighbor has twice recommended the unemployed man for job openings in companies where he has business connections. In both cases, the man who was out of work refused to call about the positions because they didn't pay enough and he felt they were "beneath him".

Now months have paste, the unemployed man has approached his neighbors asking to borrow money to pay their delinquent mortgage. He is promising to pay it back with interest.

What should they do?

- *We accept personal responsibility for our choices.*
- *Will my action or inaction harm anyone or anything?*
- *Does it take into account all that will be affected?*
- *Are any punished or rewarded unjustly?*
- *Is our motivation based on truth, fairness and reason?*
- *Does it serve the greater good?*
- *Does it sacrifice the future for an immediate goal?*
- *Are you proud of your decision?*
- *If the roles were reversed, would you be satisfied?*
- *How can my decision be reversed or remedied if I'm wrong?*

SCENARIO #41

A salesman has a problem.

His company builds very sophisticated, custom engineered solutions. It takes 10 to 12 weeks to typically design and build a system.

The client says he can have the order if his company can have his system on site in 9 weeks. With the time it will take to ship, that means it would have to be on the truck at the factory ready to go in 8 weeks.

He knows they can't make that kind of a date but they should be able to come close. His boss wants this order and has instructed him to lie to the client to get the order knowing that if they are a week late, or debugging in the field it will be too late for the client to cancel and go elsewhere.

He knows that his competition cannot build a system any faster but that they have used this tactic of lying to get the order in the past. He assumes they will again whether he does or not.

What does he do next?

- We accept personal responsibility for our choices.
- Will my action or inaction harm anyone or anything?
- Does it take into account all that will be affected?
- Are any punished or rewarded unjustly?
- Is our motivation based on truth, fairness and reason?
- Does it serve the greater good?
- Does it sacrifice the future for an immediate goal?
- Are you proud of your decision?
- If the roles were reversed, would you be satisfied?
- How can my decision be reversed or remedied if I'm wrong?

SCENARIO #42

A young man is faced with a dilemma.

He wants to ask his girl friend to marry him. She is the only daughter of wealthy parents. In anticipation of asking her, he purchased a small but high quality diamond engagement ring. It is as costly as he can afford.

He had planned to ask her to marry him on New Year's Eve but at Christmas, her parents have given her a large, very expensive diamond cocktail ring that dwarfs the one he has purchased.

He has an antique gold pocket watch, his only legacy from his grandfather. If he sells it – he can afford a much larger stone to give her than the one he has now.

What does he do next?

- *We accept personal responsibility for our choices.*
- *Will my action or inaction harm anyone or anything?*
- *Does it take into account all that will be affected?*
- *Are any punished or rewarded unjustly?*
- *Is our motivation based on truth, fairness and reason?*
- *Does it serve the greater good?*
- *Does it sacrifice the future for an immediate goal?*
- *Are you proud of your decision?*
- *If the roles were reversed, would you be satisfied?*
- *How can my decision be reversed or remedied if I'm wrong?*

SCENARIO #43

A recently hired bookkeeper at a large wholesale company has noticed a few odd discrepancies, which she shows to her co-worker, an older woman who has been with the company for over twenty years.

Apparently she can't seem to locate some merchandise which was designated as damaged in shipping. There are also a few warranty dates that don't agree and a couple of manual inventory adjustments that weren't annotated properly...

Her co-worker takes one look and advises her to forget she found anything. "Just do your job and don't look for trouble" is her response.

The new bookkeeper thought she was doing her job... what does she do now?

- *We accept personal responsibility for our choices.*
- *Will my action or inaction harm anyone or anything?*
- *Does it take into account all that will be affected?*
- *Are any punished or rewarded unjustly?*
- *Is our motivation based on truth, fairness and reason?*
- *Does it serve the greater good?*
- *Does it sacrifice the future for an immediate goal?*
- *Are you proud of your decision?*
- *If the roles were reversed, would you be satisfied?*
- *How can my decision be reversed or remedied if I'm wrong?*

SCENARIO #44

A freshman at college gives her roommate permission to type up some work for a class on her computer since the other girl's unit is being serviced.

She goes out and when she returns to her dorm room she finds that her roommate has used her computer to download some copyrighted music without paying for it.

She is concerned because the illegal downloads were made on her laptop.

Up until now, the roommates have gotten along just great. They haven't had any problems and in fact, they have been a big help several times to one another.

What should she do now?

- *We accept personal responsibility for our choices.*
- *Will my action or inaction harm anyone or anything?*
- *Does it take into account all that will be affected?*
- *Are any punished or rewarded unjustly?*
- *Is our motivation based on truth, fairness and reason?*
- *Does it serve the greater good?*
- *Does it sacrifice the future for an immediate goal?*
- *Are you proud of your decision?*
- *If the roles were reversed, would you be satisfied?*
- *How can my decision be reversed or remedied if I'm wrong?*

SCENARIO #45

A young man gets a job painting a house, because he has a reputation for doing excellent work. It is a big job and good money but while he is working – he gets an opportunity to pick up two more jobs.

Since the work of house painting is dependent on the weather, he needs to grab a job whenever he can get it.

He hires an old friend to help him out, but when he takes a break to check on the other man's work, he is shocked to see the quality of the work his assistant has done.

It doesn't look bad but it is below his very high standards. To do it the way he wants it done, whole sections will have to be cleaned and repainted. Instead of saving on the job – it would now cost him significant time and money to fix it.

What should our painter do?

- *We accept personal responsibility for our choices.*
- *Will my action or inaction harm anyone or anything?*
- *Does it take into account all that will be affected?*
- *Are any punished or rewarded unjustly?*
- *Is our motivation based on truth, fairness and reason?*
- *Does it serve the greater good?*
- *Does it sacrifice the future for an immediate goal?*
- *Are you proud of your decision?*
- *If the roles were reversed, would you be satisfied?*
- *How can my decision be reversed or remedied if I'm wrong?*

SCENARIO #46

A man is an hourly employee at a tiny company and works hard to make ends meet. His employer appreciates all that he does but does not have enough work to hire additional help. They must depend on each other.

The man gets a notice for jury service. If he gets placed on a long trial, he may lose his job because his boss can't afford to be without a helper for very long and the small stipend that jury service pays would wipe him out financially.

His boss tells him, "If you get selected just lie and tell them you are a bigot – they will excuse you".

The man doesn't want to do that but what else can he do?

- We accept personal responsibility for our choices.
- Will my action or inaction harm anyone or anything?
- Does it take into account all that will be affected?
- Are any punished or rewarded unjustly?
- Is our motivation based on truth, fairness and reason?
- Does it serve the greater good?
- Does it sacrifice the future for an immediate goal?
- Are you proud of your decision?
- If the roles were reversed, would you be satisfied?
- How can my decision be reversed or remedied if I'm wrong?

SCENARIO #47

A man moves into a small apartment that has no air conditioning.

On hot summer evenings he wants to leave his windows open but he can see into surrounding apartments and they can see him.

His neighbors don't seem to value their privacy, at least not in the same way he does and they make no effort to close their blinds.

Either way, he finds himself in an extremely uncomfortable situation.

What can he do?

- *We accept personal responsibility for our choices.*
- *Will my action or inaction harm anyone or anything?*
- *Does it take into account all that will be affected?*
- *Are any punished or rewarded unjustly?*
- *Is our motivation based on truth, fairness and reason?*
- *Does it serve the greater good?*
- *Does it sacrifice the future for an immediate goal?*
- *Are you proud of your decision?*
- *If the roles were reversed, would you be satisfied?*
- *How can my decision be reversed or remedied if I'm wrong?*

SCENARIO #48

A man makes a promise to his wife to give up smoking and keeps it – for 14 months.

While entertaining one of their largest accounts on a business trip, after dinner the client asks him to accompany him to a cigar bar. This is one of his company's biggest clients and he does not want to risk the business by declining the invitation.

Once there the customer offers him a fine cigar and the opportunity to chat in depth about how to expand the business their companies are doing.

What should he do next?

- *We accept personal responsibility for our choices.*
- *Will my action or inaction harm anyone or anything?*
- *Does it take into account all that will be affected?*
- *Are any punished or rewarded unjustly?*
- *Is our motivation based on truth, fairness and reason?*
- *Does it serve the greater good?*
- *Does it sacrifice the future for an immediate goal?*
- *Are you proud of your decision?*
- *If the roles were reversed, would you be satisfied?*
- *How can my decision be reversed or remedied if I'm wrong?*

SCENARIO #49

A teenager is treated very badly by a local shop owner.

On a chilly afternoon, the teen had entered the store while waiting for some friends. The man ejected him from the store after a few minutes while he wandered around the shop just looking at the merchandise. The owner accused him of "hanging around the store because he was trying to shoplift."

When his friends arrive and he relates the story, one of his companions suggests that they "teach the man a lesson."

What should he do next?

- We accept personal responsibility for our choices.
- Will my action or inaction harm anyone or anything?
- Does it take into account all that will be affected?
- Are any punished or rewarded unjustly?
- Is our motivation based on truth, fairness and reason?
- Does it serve the greater good?
- Does it sacrifice the future for an immediate goal?
- Are you proud of your decision?
- If the roles were reversed, would you be satisfied?
- How can my decision be reversed or remedied if I'm wrong?

SCENARIO #50

Two farmers are arguing.

At the extreme edge of farmer #1's property, he had planted corn which was ready for harvesting.

When he arrives to gather the crop, he finds that farmer #2 has already harvested the corn claiming that it is on his land.

After checking, farmer #1 sees that he had indeed accidentally planted on a small parcel of land belonging to his neighbor, but the seed, water, fertilizer and labor were all supplied by him.

What can or should be done?

- We accept personal responsibility for our choices.
- Will my action or inaction harm anyone or anything?
- Does it take into account all that will be affected?
- Are any punished or rewarded unjustly?
- Is our motivation based on truth, fairness and reason?
- Does it serve the greater good?
- Does it sacrifice the future for an immediate goal?
- Are you proud of your decision?
- If the roles were reversed, would you be satisfied?
- How can my decision be reversed or remedied if I'm wrong?

SCENARIO #51

A young man's older brother leaves for college.

When he returns, the younger man hears his brother repeatedly making racist jokes and comments that he finds shocking and very offensive. He has never heard or seen his brother behave in this manner before.

He loves his brother and he has missed him since he has been gone but cannot understand what has happened to change him in this way.

What does he do now?

- *We accept personal responsibility for our choices.*
- *Will my action or inaction harm anyone or anything?*
- *Does it take into account all that will be affected?*
- *Are any punished or rewarded unjustly?*
- *Is our motivation based on truth, fairness and reason?*
- *Does it serve the greater good?*
- *Does it sacrifice the future for an immediate goal?*
- *Are you proud of your decision?*
- *If the roles were reversed, would you be satisfied?*
- *How can my decision be reversed or remedied if I'm wrong?*

SCENARIO #52

A sales person has worked for a company for seven years when the firm lands upon hard times. Although she continues to put in long hours – the results are meager.

Despite this, it is common knowledge that the owner continues to take cash out of the company in the form of large bonuses paid to himself.

One day, the owner comes to the salesperson without warning and fires her citing the current downturn in business as the reason. She is given no severance and asked to leave the premises immediately.

After she has left, she finds copies of her old working files on her home computer including some sensitive data such as customer records and pricing information.

She might be able to use this information to get a job with a competitor or start her own business. Although discussed, her previous company did not have an employee agreement with her.

What should she do?

The Un-Official Answer Key

The employment of ethics is often more complicated that a simple right and wrong – good and bad – black and white.

The goal of this work is to elicit discussion.

The purpose of this "answer key" is to help bring the participants to a conclusion and occasionally illuminate points that may have been overlooked.

1 – Did you consider in your deliberations that it is not your kidney to give away?

2 – Others will do what they will do and think what they will think. Take the bag to the police and tell them the truth.

3 – If you wouldn't buy it, knowing what you know – why would you sell it without giving the other man that same knowledge to make an informed decision?

4 – What kind of a sound future can be built based on keeping secrets?

5 – Grudges are among the heaviest burdens we can carry. She must talk to him non-confrontationally or forever be nagged by worry and doubt.

6 – The specification was written for a reason. Someone chose to ignore it for a reason. Find out the truth of the matter and fix the discrepancy.

7 – That rule exists for the safety of all. Obey the rule and do not be afraid to say why. You may find others were waiting for someone to speak up.

8 – Voting for someone based on a single issue is like buying a car because it has one good tire. Cast your vote for people who share your ethics. The likelihood is that they will best represent your conscience.

9 – He must bear the consequences of his failure or he will think there are no consequences for failure. Possessing talent in one area does not excuse bad behavior in another. Quite the contrary, it should make us all the more responsible for what we do.

10 – Bend a hook into a unique shape and tag the fish through the dorsal. Let any who doubt you land the fish to disprove your story. If they doubt it – the truth is still the truth and the knowledge of that should be enough to satisfy the fisherman.

11 – He should go to the police and admit his error – or it may be compounded by not reporting it.

12 - It is the obligation of the doctor to heal; it is the obligation of the attorney to be an agent for justice under the law based on the oaths they both took when they began their career. If either person denies the true calling of their profession - the young girl will be doomed.

13 - The officer is obligated to see that everyone, including the prosecutor adheres to the law. The prosecutor may have misinterpreted something or made a mistake. He should talk to him about his concerns. They both want to see the right person punished, not to have an innocent man convicted wrongly or a guilty one released on a technicality.

14 - No matter how noble, she cannot give away what does not belong to her. The baker is not purposely heartless – he used to donate the food. He is merely afraid because of a past incident. She should seek to bring the baker and the head of the soup kitchen together to see if they can resolve it.

15 - Regardless of his personal situation, if the homeless man fails to stop one of the police and report what he has seen, opting to wait and recover the purse later – he no longer just looks like the thief, he becomes a thief.

16 - He should stop the donor if he can and ask if he meant to be so generous or was it a mistake? If it was a mistake, the donor can make a decision to let it be or take it back. If it was his intention to donate it, knowing the coin's value, it belongs to the charity.

17 - It is a painful lesson, but the couple made a mistake in accepting the bills without checking. Passing them again simply extends the pain to others and makes them just as guilty as the person who cheated them.

18 - The boy's family is almost certainly waiting. What happens next is their decision. No one should take that away from them.

19 - Two wrongs do not make a right. The programmer cannot take matters into her own hands. She has various legal means to get what is owed her. If she damages or disrupts the client's system, she too is in the wrong.

20 - Qui tacet consentit, "Silence gives consent". The longer he waits to speak up, the less likely he is to be believed and the greater the damage that will occur.

21 - If the man's time is more precious than resolving his service issue at this moment, he has a remedy. He can leave and return later but the clerk's lack of experience and absence of people to help her does not give the customer license to berate her. You should speak up and say so.

22 - If he would not invest his own money, he cannot in good conscience advise others to do so.

23 - Should not does not mean – *can not*. If he does not trust the mechanic, he should take it to another shop for their opinion, even if it must be towed. That is not an accusation and should not be treated as such, by either party.

24 - Loyalty to his friend is admirable – but his employer and other co-workers are due a measure of loyalty as well. If the foreman feels an obligation to his friend, he cannot ask the others to repay that obligation for him... The friend should go.

25 - True friends give each other what they need – even when they don't want it. She is asking for help, get help for her...

26 - If you are worried what your parents or others might think, maybe there is a good reason they would object. Go slow and not fear the opinion of others. Give important decisions the consideration they deserve. Ethical decisions should not have to fear the light of day.

27 - Trading your future for today is never a good deal and why would you trust your future to have different interests at heart?

28 - You should never be too busy to do the right thing. Justice delayed is justice denied.

29 – When you are falsely accused, your only defenses are your reputation and the truth. Your ethics are the guardian of both, that is why you must maintain them.

30 - Your ethics should be cast in concrete, not your mistakes. Substandard work will follow you.

31 – This has nothing to do with a "team". It has to do with being made a scapegoat. If you do not stand up for the truth of the matter, you will become a victim by choice.

32 - Things change. You do not own the establishment and cannot dictate conditions to the owner but you can take your business elsewhere. You can choose who you associate with.

33 – You cannot take the kittens home without parental consent but you may be able to offer assistance to place them rather than see them put to sleep. Living our principles in real world situations often involves seeking creative solutions.

34 – There would be no moral dilemma if the company president felt the potential investor had the best interests of his people at heart. The fact that he is worried speaks volumes. Find the money elsewhere.

35 – Qualities like friendship, loyalty and respect should never be traded for anything less than qualities like friendship, loyalty and respect.

36 – We are all the product of our choices. If you make sound choices, why would you be ashamed of who you are or what you do?

37 – If something is wrong, it is wrong. Explain your situation and ask for other work there until you are old enough to wait tables.

38 – Your best friend has a demonstrated history with you. Why would you give that up, particularly for people who do not value that?

39 - Give the new man a chance, there may be another reason for the hire you are unaware of. However, if your opinion of his unsuitability remains unchanged for sound reasons, you can

protest the matter to upper management but keep personalities out of it or your motives will be suspect.

40 – Lending him the money will only encourage further "bad" behavior. You may continue to assist them in other ways but are not obligated to lend them money.

41 – Tell the truth. Explain how you can compress the time frame but set an appropriate level of expectation. If you suspect your competitor will lie about deliver – encourage your client to contact companies where you know this to be the case.

42 – Talk to the prospective fiancé. You cannot "keep up" with her wealthy parents and you cannot "buy" love. Now is the time to find out where her heart is.

43 – You cannot remain there in silence and not be complicit. If upper management is involved – get out, fast.

44 – She should pay for the music and tell the roommate she has done so. Explain to the other girl that her good name was placed in jeopardy by misuse of a computer registered to her. The roommate should apologize and make restitution, regardless she might want to change her password.

45 – When the painter hired an assistant, he extended his reputation to cover him. He was responsible to insure that the work was done up to his standards. He must absorb the loss and re-do the job or sacrifice his good name.

46 – Don't lie. Explain your economic situation. The judge is a person too.

47 - Buy an inexpensive window fan and close the blinds. Sometimes we over think these things.

48 – Accept the invitation to sit and talk business, but decline the cigar. Explain about your promise. Your customer might be impressed that you keep your word.

49 – It all depends on the lesson. If they seek to punish the man by stealing his stock, damaging his store or injuring him – the lesson he will learn is that he was right; teenagers are no good. Behaving ethically, they have the opportunity to show the shopkeeper that he was wrong about them and that they are good people. That is the better lesson for all parties.

50 – Technically farmer #1 was trespassing, however forfeiting the entire crop would unjustly enrich farmer #2 (who must have known the field had been planted and he didn't do it. Otherwise he would not have known to harvest it). Ethically, the two men should work out an equitable split of the value.

51 – If, as the young man says he doesn't understand – he should talk to his brother. There is nothing wrong with saying I don't think that joke is funny or appropriate. Loving a person does not obligate you to condone their unethical behavior. If we work from the position that a lack of ethics is destructive in nature, caring about a person requires that we say something, doesn't it?

52 – As tempting as it might be, the information is not hers and should be erased.

www.ingramcontent.com/pod-product-compliance
Lightning Source LLC
Chambersburg PA
CBHW031400040426
42444CB00005B/365